An Illustrated Timeline of
U.S. STATES

by Patricia Wooster

illustrated by Rick Morgan

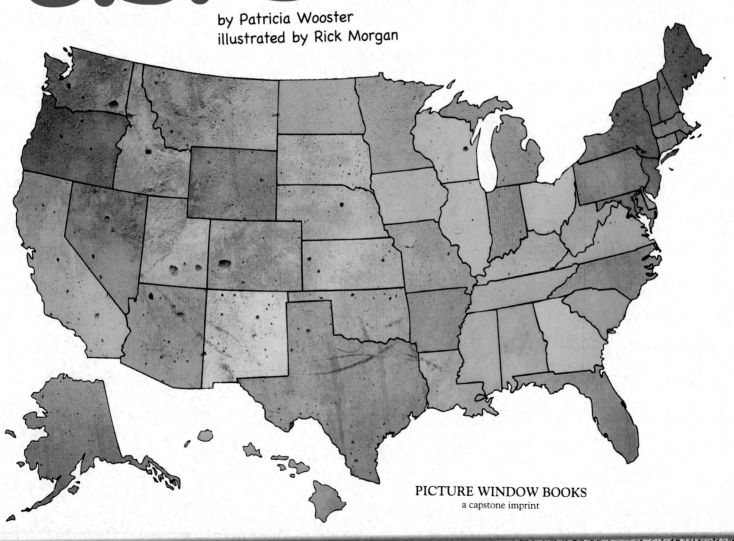

PICTURE WINDOW BOOKS

a capstone imprint

Special thanks to our adviser, Terry Flaherty, PhD, Professor of English,
Minnesota State University, Mankato, for his expertise.

Editor: Jill Kalz
Designer: Tracy Davies
Art Director: Nathan Gassman
Production Specialist: Sarah Bennett
The illustrations in this book were created with pencil and digital color.

Photo Credits: Photo Credits: Shutterstock: Andrew Chin, Beta Becla, Christopher Poliquin,
David M. Schrader, leigh, MaxFX, Philip Lange, Richard Laschon, SeDmi, Stacie Stauff
Smith Photography, Subbotina Anna

Picture Window Books
1710 Roe Crest Drive
North Mankato, MN 56003
www.capstonepub.com

Library of Congress Cataloging-in-Publication Data
Wooster, Patricia.
 An illustrated timeline of U.S. States / by Patricia Wooster ;
illustrated by Rick Morgan.
    p. cm. — (Visual timelines in history)
 Includes index.
 ISBN 978-1-4048-6663-8 (library binding)
 ISBN 978-1-4048-7020-8 (paperback)
 1. U.S. States—History—Chronology—Juvenile literature. 2. United
States—History—Chronology—Juvenile literature. I. Morgan, Rick,
1954- ill. II. Title.
 E174.5.W66 2012
 973—dc22
                        2011010469

Printed in the United States of America in Eau Claire, Wisconsin.
010319   001465

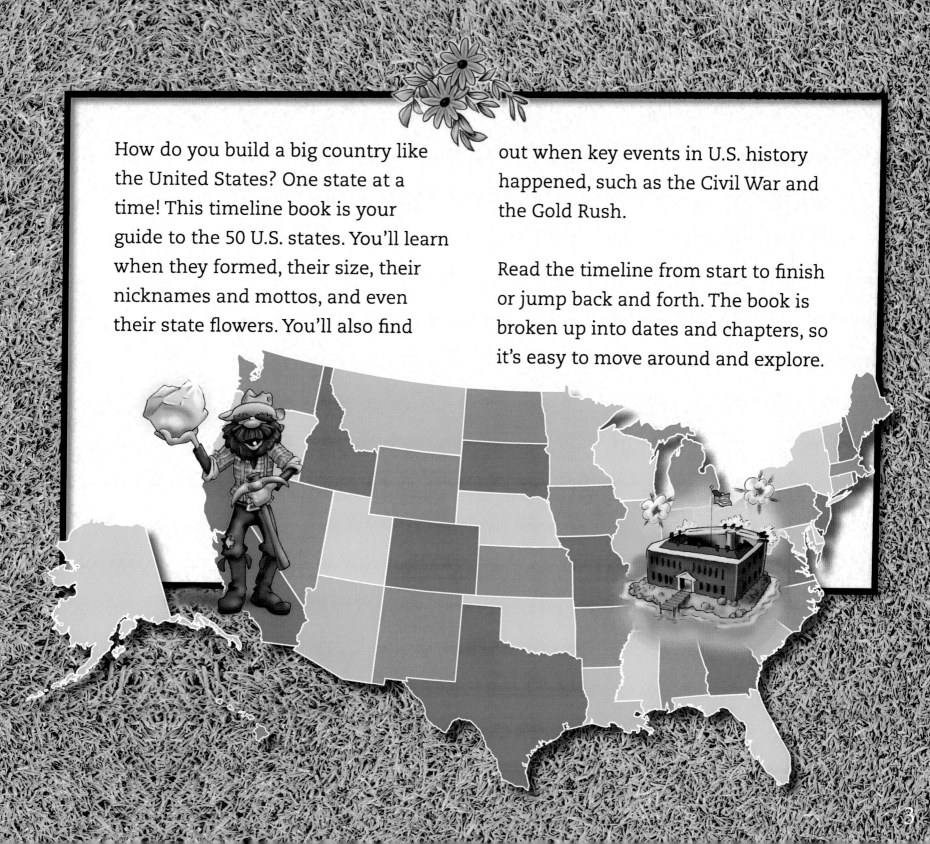

How do you build a big country like the United States? One state at a time! This timeline book is your guide to the 50 U.S. states. You'll learn when they formed, their size, their nicknames and mottos, and even their state flowers. You'll also find out when key events in U.S. history happened, such as the Civil War and the Gold Rush.

Read the timeline from start to finish or jump back and forth. The book is broken up into dates and chapters, so it's easy to move around and explore.

BIRTH OF A NATION

April 2, 1513

Juan Ponce de León discovers what is now Florida. He claims the land for Spain.

December 20, 1620

The Pilgrims settle in Plymouth, Massachusetts. They have arrived from England aboard the *Mayflower*.

May 14, 1607

The first English settlement is established at Jamestown, Virginia.

1655

Settlers purchase part of present-day Long Island, New York, from the Montauk Indians.

July 4, 1776

The United States approves the Declaration of Independence. By doing so, it claims its freedom from Great Britain.

April 19, 1775

The Revolutionary War between the American Colonies and Great Britain begins.

THE FIRST U.S. STATES

September 3, 1783

The Paris Peace Treaty is signed. The Revolutionary War ends, and the United States becomes a free nation.

December 7, 1787

Delaware becomes the first U.S. state. It is also the first to ratify the U.S. Constitution.

NICKNAME: First State
AREA: 2,489 sq. miles
POPULATION: 897,934
STATE MOTTO: Liberty and Independence
STATE FLOWER: Peach Blossom

December 12, 1787

Pennsylvania, 2nd state
NICKNAME: Keystone State
AREA: 46,055 sq. miles
POPULATION: 12,702,379
STATE MOTTO: Virtue, Liberty, and Independence
STATE FLOWER: Mountain Laurel

December 18, 1787

New Jersey, 3rd state
NICKNAME: Garden State
AREA: 8,721 sq. miles
POPULATION: 8,791,894
STATE MOTTO: Liberty and Prosperity
STATE FLOWER: Common Meadow Violet

EIGHT STATES IN ONE YEAR

January 2, 1788

Georgia, 4th state
NICKNAME: Peach State
AREA: 59,425 sq. miles
POPULATION: 9,687,653
STATE MOTTO: Wisdom, Justice, and Moderation
STATE FLOWER: Cherokee Rose

February 6, 1788

Massachusetts, 6th state
NICKNAME: Bay State
AREA: 10,555 sq. miles; **POPULATION:** 6,547,629
STATE MOTTO: By the Sword We Seek Peace, But Peace Only Under Liberty
STATE FLOWER: Mayflower

January 9, 1788

Connecticut, 5th state
NICKNAME: Constitution State
AREA: 5,543 sq. miles; **POPULATION:** 3,574,097
STATE MOTTO: He Who Transplanted Still Sustains
STATE FLOWER: Mountain Laurel

April 28, 1788

Maryland, 7th state
NICKNAME: Old Line State
AREA: 12,407 sq. miles
POPULATION: 5,773,552
STATE MOTTO: Manly Deeds, Womanly Words
STATE FLOWER: Black-eyed Susan

May 23, 1788

South Carolina,
8th state
NICKNAME:
Palmetto State
AREA: 32,020 sq. miles
POPULATION: 4,625,364
STATE MOTTOS: While I
Breathe, I Hope; Ready
in Soul and Resource
STATE FLOWER: Yellow Jessamine

June 25, 1788

Virginia, 10th state
NICKNAME: Old Dominion
AREA: 42,774 sq. miles
POPULATION: 8,001,024
STATE MOTTO: Thus Always to Tyrants
STATE FLOWER: American Dogwood

June 21, 1788

New Hampshire,
9th state
NICKNAME: Granite State
AREA: 9,350 sq. miles
POPULATION: 1,316,470
STATE MOTTO: Live Free
or Die
STATE FLOWER: Purple Lilac

July 26, 1788

New York, 11th state
NICKNAME: Empire State
AREA: 54,556 sq. miles; **POPULATION:** 19,378,102
STATE MOTTO: Ever Upward; **STATE FLOWER:** Rose

ELECTING THE FIRST LEADERS

May 29, 1790

Rhode Island,
13th state
NICKNAME: Ocean State
AREA: 1,545 sq. miles
POPULATION: 1,052,567
STATE MOTTO: Hope
STATE FLOWER: Violet

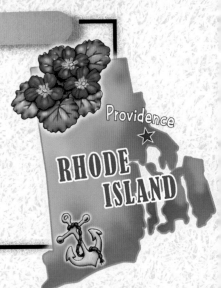

Providence ★

RHODE ISLAND

▶ April 30, 1789

George Washington
is sworn in as the
first president of the
United States.

RALEIGH ★

NORTH CAROLINA

November 21, 1789

North Carolina, 12th state
NICKNAME: Tar Heel State; **AREA:** 53,819 sq. miles
POPULATION: 9,535,483; **STATE MOTTO:** To Be, Rather
Than to Seem; **STATE FLOWER:** Dogwood

March 4, 1791

Vermont, 14th state
NICKNAME: Green
Mountain State
AREA: 9,614 sq. miles
POPULATION: 625,741
STATE MOTTO: Freedom
and Unity
STATE FLOWER: Red Clover

MONTPELIER ★

VERMONT

December 15, 1791

The Bill of Rights becomes part of the U.S. Constitution. These 10 changes, or amendments, to the Constitution state the basic rights of all U.S. citizens.

June 1, 1796

Tennessee, 16th state
NICKNAME: Volunteer State
AREA: 42,143 sq. miles; **POPULATION:** 6,346,105
STATE MOTTO: Agriculture and Commerce
STATE FLOWER: Iris

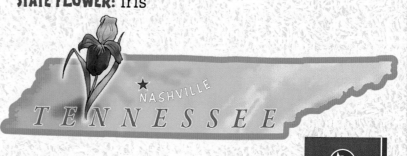

NASHVILLE

TENNESSEE

June 1, 1792

FRANKFORT

Kentucky

Kentucky, 15th state
NICKNAME: Bluegrass State
AREA: 40,409 sq. miles; **POPULATION:** 4,339,367
STATE MOTTO: United We Stand, Divided We Fall
STATE FLOWER: Goldenrod

November 3, 1796

John Adams is elected the second president of the United States.

11

NEW TERRITORIES

June 11, 1800

The U.S. capital completes its move from Philadelphia, Pennsylvania, to Washington, D.C. New York City had been the site of the first U.S. capital, followed by Philadelphia in December 1790.

March 1, 1803

Ohio, 17th state
NICKNAME: Buckeye State
AREA: 44,825 sq. miles
POPULATION: 11,536,504
STATE MOTTO: With God, All Things Are Possible
STATE FLOWER: Scarlet Carnation

Ohio
★
COLUMBUS

April 30, 1803

The United States makes the Louisiana Purchase from France. The deal is $15 million for all or part of 15 current U.S. states.

May 14, 1804

Meriwether Lewis and William Clark begin traveling up the Missouri River. They will go on to reach the Pacific Ocean in November 1805.

April 30, 1812

Louisiana, 18th state
NICKNAME: Pelican State
AREA: 51,840 sq. miles
POPULATION: 4,533,372
STATE MOTTO: Union, Justice, Confidence
STATE FLOWER: Magnolia

December 22, 1807

The Embargo Act stops all trade between the United States and other countries.

June 18, 1812

The War of 1812 begins. The United States and Great Britain fight mostly over trade limits and control of the seas. The Treaty of Ghent officially ends the war in 1814, but fighting goes into 1815.

MARKING 50 YEARS AS A NATION

December 11, 1816

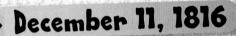 

Indiana, 19th state
NICKNAME: Hoosier State
AREA: 36,418 sq. miles; **POPULATION:** 6,483,802
STATE MOTTO: The Crossroads of America
STATE FLOWER: Peony

December 10, 1817

Mississippi,
20th state
NICKNAME:
Magnolia State
AREA: 48,430 sq. miles
POPULATION: 2,967,297
STATE MOTTO: By Valor
and Arms
STATE FLOWER: Magnolia

December 3, 1818

Illinois, 21st state
NICKNAME:
Prairie State
AREA: 57,914 sq. miles
POPULATION: 12,830,632
STATE MOTTO: State
Sovereignty, National Union
STATE FLOWER: Purple Violet

December 14, 1819

Alabama, 22nd state
NICKNAME: Heart
of Dixie
AREA: 52,419 sq. miles
POPULATION: 4,779,736
STATE MOTTO: We Dare
Defend Our Rights
STATE FLOWER: Camellia

August 10, 1821

Missouri, 24th state
NICKNAME: Show Me State; **AREA:** 69,704 sq. miles
POPULATION: 5,988,927
STATE MOTTO: Let the
Welfare of the People
Be the Supreme Law
STATE FLOWER: Hawthorn

March 15, 1820

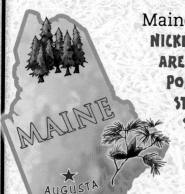

Maine, 23rd state
NICKNAME: Pine Tree State
AREA: 35,385 sq. miles
POPULATION: 1,328,361
STATE MOTTO: I Lead
STATE FLOWER: White Pine
Cone and Tassel

December 2, 1823

The Monroe Doctrine warns
European countries against
colonizing land in North
or South America.

ADDING MORE LAND

▶ **June 30, 1834**

The Indian Territory is set aside as a place for American Indians to live and trade. It includes a large area west of the Mississippi River that is later reduced to the size of present-day Oklahoma.

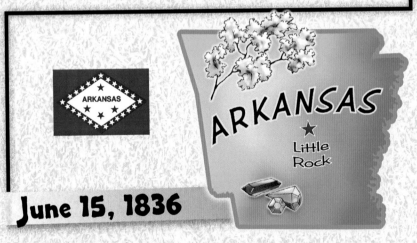

June 15, 1836

Arkansas, 25th state
NICKNAME: Natural State; **AREA:** 53,179 sq. miles
POPULATION: 2,915,918; **STATE MOTTO:** The People Rule
STATE FLOWER: Apple Blossom

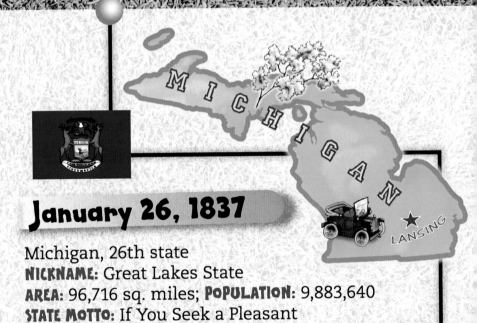

January 26, 1837

Michigan, 26th state
NICKNAME: Great Lakes State
AREA: 96,716 sq. miles; **POPULATION:** 9,883,640
STATE MOTTO: If You Seek a Pleasant Peninsula, Look About You
STATE FLOWER: Apple Blossom

1838

The Cherokee nation is forced to leave its homeland east of the Mississippi River and move to modern-day Oklahoma. The movement is known as the Trail of Tears.

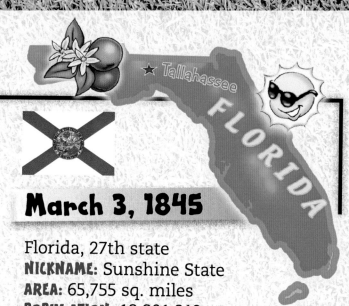

March 3, 1845

Florida, 27th state
NICKNAME: Sunshine State
AREA: 65,755 sq. miles
POPULATION: 18,801,310
STATE MOTTO: In God We Trust
STATE FLOWER: Orange Blossom

April 12, 1844

The Republic of Texas (highlighted in gold) asks to be annexed by the United States but is turned down. It asks again in 1845 and is successful.

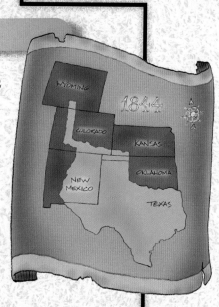

December 29, 1845

Texas, 28th state
NICKNAME: Lone Star State
AREA: 268,581 sq. miles
POPULATION: 25,145,561; **STATE MOTTO:** Friendship
STATE FLOWER: Bluebonnet

THE PUSH WEST

December 28, 1846

Iowa, 29th state
NICKNAME: Hawkeye State
AREA: 56,272 sq. miles; **POPULATION:** 3,046,355
STATE MOTTO: Our Liberties We Prize and Our Rights We Will Maintain
STATE FLOWER: Wild Prairie Rose

January 24, 1848

James Wilson Marshall discovers gold in present-day California. Thousands of people flock to the area to take part in the Gold Rush.

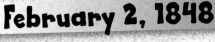

February 2, 1848

The Mexican-American War ends. The United States gains land that will become California, Nevada, Utah, and parts of Arizona, Colorado, New Mexico, and Wyoming.

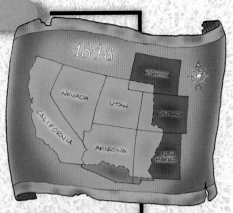

May 29, 1848

Wisconsin, 30th state
NICKNAME: Badger State
AREA: 65,498 sq. miles
POPULATION: 5,686,986
STATE MOTTO: Forward
STATE FLOWER: Wood Violet

September 9, 1850

California, 31st state
NICKNAME: Golden State
AREA: 163,696 sq. miles
POPULATION: 37,253,956
STATE MOTTO: Eureka
(I Have Found It)
STATE FLOWER: Golden Poppy

August 14, 1848

The United States annexes the Oregon Territory. The area includes present-day Idaho, Washington, and Oregon, and part of Montana and Wyoming.

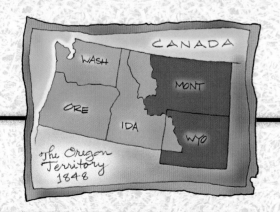

The Oregon Territory 1848

May 11, 1858

Minnesota, 32nd state
NICKNAME: Land of 10,000 Lakes
AREA: 86,939 sq. miles
POPULATION: 5,303,925
STATE MOTTO: The Star of the North
STATE FLOWER: Lady Slipper

19

A NATION DIVIDED

▶ February 14, 1859

Oregon, 33rd state
NICKNAME: Beaver State
AREA: 98,381 sq. miles
POPULATION: 3,831,074
STATE MOTTO: She Flies with Her Own Wings
STATE FLOWER: Oregon Grape

January 29, 1861

Kansas, 34th state
NICKNAME: Sunflower State
AREA: 82,277 sq. miles; **POPULATION:** 2,853,118
STATE MOTTO: To the Stars Through Difficulties
STATE FLOWER: Sunflower

December 20, 1860

South Carolina secedes from, or leaves, the United States. Ten other states will soon join it to become the Confederate States of America.

April 12, 1861

Shots are fired at Fort Sumter, South Carolina. The Civil War begins between the North (the Union) and South (the Confederate States of America).

WEST VIRGINIA
★ CHARLESTON

June 20, 1863

West Virginia, 35th state
NICKNAME: Mountain State
AREA: 24,230 sq. miles
POPULATION: 1,852,994
STATE MOTTO: Mountaineers Are Always Free
STATE FLOWER: Rhododendron

April 9, 1865

The Confederate States of America surrender to the Union. The Civil War ends.

October 31, 1864

Nevada, 36th state
NICKNAME: Silver State
AREA: 110,561 sq. miles
POPULATION: 2,700,551
STATE MOTTO: All for Our Country
STATE FLOWER: Sagebrush

NEVADA
★ CARSON CITY

July 24, 1866

Tennessee becomes the first state readmitted into the Union. The other 10 states of the former confederacy will follow. Georgia will return last, in July 1870.

UNITED AGAIN AND GROWING

▶ March 1, 1867

Nebraska, 37th state
NICKNAME: Cornhusker State
AREA: 77,354 sq. miles; **POPULATION:** 1,826,341
STATE MOTTO: Equality before the Law
STATE FLOWER: Goldenrod

NEBRASKA

LINCOLN ★

DENVER ★

Colorado

August 1, 1876

Colorado, 38th state
NICKNAME: Centennial State
AREA: 104,094 sq. miles; **POPULATION:** 5,029,196
STATE MOTTO: Nothing without Providence
STATE FLOWER: Rocky Mountain Columbine

The Times

3¢

SEWARD'S FOLLY

ALASKA PURCHASED FROM RUSSIA FOR $7.2 MILLION

March 30, 1867

The United States purchases the Alaska Territory from Russia for $7.2 million.

November 2, 1889

North Dakota, 39th state
NICKNAME: Peace Garden State
AREA: 70,700 sq. miles; **POPULATION:** 672,591
STATE MOTTO: Liberty and Union, Now and Forever,
One and Inseparable
STATE FLOWER: Wild Prairie Rose

November 8, 1889

Montana, 41st state
NICKNAME: Treasure State
AREA: 147,042 sq. miles; **POPULATION:** 989,415
STATE MOTTO: Gold and Silver
STATE FLOWER: Bitterroot

November 2, 1889

South Dakota, 40th state
NICKNAME: Mount Rushmore State
AREA: 77,116 sq. miles; **POPULATION:** 814,180
STATE MOTTO: Under God the People Rule
STATE FLOWER: American Pasqueflower

November 11, 1889

Washington, 42nd state
NICKNAME: Evergreen State
AREA: 71,300 sq. miles
POPULATION: 6,724,540; **STATE MOTTO:** By and By
STATE FLOWER: Coast Rhododendron

EXPANDING TO THE ISLANDS

July 3, 1890

Idaho, 43rd state
NICKNAME: Gem State
AREA: 83,570 sq. miles
POPULATION: 1,567,582
STATE MOTTO: Let It Be Perpetual
STATE FLOWER: Syringa

July 10, 1890

Wyoming, 44th state
NICKNAME: Cowboy State; **AREA:** 97,814 sq. miles
POPULATION: 563,626; **STATE MOTTO:** Equal Rights
STATE FLOWER: Indian Paintbrush

January 4, 1896

Utah, 45th state
NICKNAME: Beehive State
AREA: 84,899 sq. miles
POPULATION: 2,763,885
STATE MOTTO: Industry
STATE FLOWER: Sego Lily

April 25, 1898

The Spanish-American War begins. Fighting centers around Cuba and its wish to be free from Spanish rule.

December 10, 1898

The United States and Spain sign the Treaty of Paris. The Spanish-American War ends. So does Spain's colonial rule in the Americas.

July 7, 1898

The United States annexes Hawaii.

February 6, 1899

The United States annexes Guam, the Philippines, and Puerto Rico.

A POPULATION MILESTONE

▶ November 6, 1903

Panama gives the United States rights to build and control the Panama Canal.

January 6, 1912

New Mexico, 47th state
NICKNAME: Land of Enchantment
AREA: 121,589 sq. miles
POPULATION: 2,059,179
STATE MOTTO: It Grows as It Goes
STATE FLOWER: Yucca

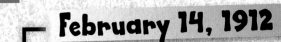

November 16, 1907

Oklahoma, 46th state
NICKNAME: Sooner State
AREA: 69,898 sq. miles; **POPULATION:** 3,751,351
STATE MOTTO: Labor Conquers All Things
STATE FLOWER: Oklahoma Rose

February 14, 1912

Arizona, 48th state
NICKNAME: Grand Canyon State
AREA: 113,998 sq. miles
POPULATION: 6,392,017
STATE MOTTO: God Enriches
STATE FLOWER: Saguaro Cactus Blossom

1915

The U.S. population reaches 100 million.

U.S. POPULATION GROWTH CHART

100,000,000

75,000,000

50,000,000

25,000,000

March 2, 1917

Puerto Rico becomes a U.S. territory.

SAN JUAN

PUERTO RICO

Welcome to U.S. Virgin Islands formerly Danish West Indies

August 4, 1916

The United States buys the Danish West Indies (St. Thomas, St. John, and St. Croix) for $25 million. The islands are later called the U.S. Virgin Islands.

THE LATEST STATES AND BEYOND

June 26, 1945

The United Nations is created. Its member countries work together for the greater good of the world.

April 4, 1949

NATO is created. Twelve countries join, including the United States.

January 3, 1959

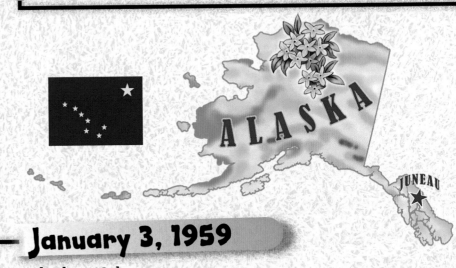

Alaska, 49th state
NICKNAME: The Last Frontier; **AREA:** 663,267 sq. miles
POPULATION: 710,231; **STATE MOTTO:** North to the Future
STATE FLOWER: Forget-me-not

U.S. POPULATION GROWTH CHART

200,000,000

100,000,000

50,000,000

25,000,000

1967

The U.S. population reaches 200 million.

300 MILLION 2006

October 17, 2006

The U.S. population reaches 300 million.

HONOLULU

Hawaii

August 21, 1959

Hawaii, 50th state
NICKNAME: Aloha State
AREA: 10,931 sq. miles; **POPULATION:** 1,360,301
STATE MOTTO: The Life of the Land Is Perpetuated in Righteousness; **STATE FLOWER:** Hibiscus

December 31, 1999

The United States returns the Panama Canal and its surrounding territory to Panama.

DEED PANAMA CANAL TO PANAMA 31 DECEMBER 1999

Uncle Sam

PANAMA

BUILD YOUR OWN TIMELINE

A timeline represents a number of events in the order in which they happened. Create a timeline based on the history of your home state.

Start with the date it became a state. Then follow its progress through the years. Include items such as the creation of the state capital, conflicts or wars, major weather events, and natural disasters. Include moments by famous people from your state, whether in politics, entertainment, or sports. A lot of this information can be found in a world almanac or your state's government web site.

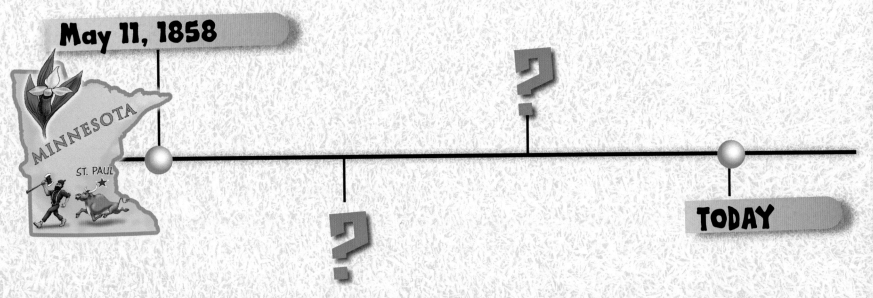

May 11, 1858

MINNESOTA

ST. PAUL

?

?

TODAY